America's Masajid & Islamic Centers
- A Pictorial Account

Amir N. Muhammad

From Collections & Stories of American Muslims 10th Anniversary

ISBN # 0-9742868-2-6

LCCN # 2006907410

FreeMan Publications
2524 Elvans Rd   SE
Washington, DC 20020

Fax # 202 678-1537

Website: www.Muslimsinamerica.org

- *Cover page: The 'Mithrab' of the Islamic Center of Washington, DC*

Bismi allah, Ar Raham, Ar Rahim

Foreword

Early Masajid *(Mosques)* in America

After researching America's Islamic history among the enslaved Muslim men and women from West Africa, we found many reports of Muslims living in America. Some have left autobiographies, while others left reports of their heroism and Islamic faith. It seems logical that among some of the early houses of prayer of the former slaves, some were places of worship for Muslims practicing at least part of their Islamic faith. There are a few signs and hints, particularly left in the south pointing to this. In Savannah, Georgia the First African Baptist Church has Arabic script written on the pews of the second floor, while a church grave yard in Mt. Pleasant, North Carolina has at least four of its founding members' tombstones with the symbol of the 'One Finger' symbolizing the oneness of G-d. The use of the 'One Finger' as a sign for G-d's oneness is an old Islamic tradition. Many Muslims world wide still use the 'One Finger' in their prayer today as a sign of Allah's (G-d's) oneness. On Sapelo Island, in Georgia it's still a tradition in church to pray towards the east and separate the males and females. Finally, we find in the narratives of Georgia's former slave reports Muslims practicing their faith, fasting and praying.

By the turn of the 20th century Masajid *(Mosques)* began to mushroom on the American landscape. Muslims from Eastern Europe began to open centers and mosques. In 1907 the Polish Tartars established a cultural center and Mosque in Brooklyn, NY. In 1915 Albanian Muslims established a Mosque in Biddeford, Maine on the grounds of the mill, and by 1919 Mosques and Islamic Centers were established in Connecticut and in the mid-west in Highland Park, Michigan; in 1924 Michigan City, Indiana; in 1925 Cedar Rapids, Iowa; in 1926 Ross, North Dakota and 1930 in Quincy, Massachusetts.

Today there are reports of more than 1,700 Masajid *(Mosques)* and Islamic Centers across America. We have been able to document more than 1,500 Masajid and Islamic Centers. Additionally, there are many hundreds of other places used throughout America for offering prayers and conducting Jumah prayer gatherings. These places range from community centers, schools, college campuses, hotels, hospitals, offices, airports, to federal buildings such as the US Capitol.

By the turn of the 21st century the Muslim community in America has grown to 7-8 million by many estimates. According to the American Muslim Council in the mid 1990s the largest Muslim ethnic group was that of the African-American who alone account for 42.0 %, followed by South Asians numbering 24.4%, Arabs 12.2%, Africans 5.2%, Iranians 3.6%, Turks 2.4%, South East Asians 2.0%, White Americans 1.6 %, East Europeans 0.8%, while others form 5.6% of the American Muslim population.

One of the things I've noted while compiling this book is that there was a 24% average increase in Masajid *(Mosques)* and Islamic Centers across the country during the last twenty five years from the mid 1980s to 2005 with some regions accounting to almost 40% growth. Yet another noteworthy observation was made that there are at least two Masjid or Islamic Centers in every state except In the state of Vermont and Hawaii which each have one Masjid and/or an Islamic Center.

The region with the most recorded Masajid and Islamic Centers is the Mid-Atlantic states, with at least four hundred and six Masajid and Islamic Centers, followed by the Southeast and South Central region with at least three hundred and ninety three Masajid and Islamic Centers. The states with the most Masajid and Islamic Centers are California with at least 200, New York with at least 162, and Texas with at least 101 Masajid. The states with fifty or more are New Jersey with 94, Illinois 81, Michigan 76, Pennsylvania 57, and Georgia 52, followed by both Ohio and North Carolina with 50 Masjid each. The cities and metropolitan areas with the largest number of Masajid or Islamic Centers in them are New York City with 91, followed by the City of Chicago with 34 within the city limits, Detroit and Dearborn with 32, Philadelphia with 23, Los Angeles with 19, and Newark, NJ; Dallas, TX; Houston, TX; and San Diego with 13 Masajid and Islamic Centers each.

Seventy four of the Masajid and Islamic Centers' photos presented in this book have been photographed by me during my research travels covering the history of Muslims in America. Five of the photos are from my wife Habeebah Muhammad's research and travels, twenty photos are contributed by Masajid and Islamic Centers across the country and four of the photos belong to Riad K. Ali Collection.

Foremost, I would like to thank G-d (Allah) the Creator of the Heavens and Earth for blessing me and making me able bodied to travel around the country and for helping me and inspiring me to produce this book. I would like to thank Hasnah Tauhidi for her many hours of work contacting the various Masajid and Imams around the country and Habeebah Muhammad for her editing services. I would also like to acknowledge the early works of the American Muslim Council, the painstaking efforts of Omar Khalidi, and Riad K. Ali with regard to the photo material and documentation concerning the history of America's Mosques, and the current works of the Pluralism Project of the University of Harvard.

Amir N. Muhammad
July 6, 2006

Introduction

Presented in this book are pictorial accounts of over 100 Masajid and Islamic Centers, which cover just a small percentage of Masajid (Mosques) and Islamic Centers across America. The pictorial depiction of these Masajid range from some of the earliest structures to the newly built ones, from inner cities to the suburbs, representing a variety of Islamic architectural styles. Many of the photos come from Amir Nashid Muhammad and Habeebah Muhammad's collection taken during the past ten years of their travels around the country, except where indicated otherwise. Some photos have been furnished by various Masajid across the country who have shown tremendous enthusiasm for this book project.

A Masjid (Mosque) is a place in which Muslims pray to Allah (G-d) and worship collectively. The Arabic word Masjid means "the place where one prostrates oneself in worship." (Mosque) is the French word for Masjid. Masajid is the plural of Masjid. Some standard features of a Mosque are a Minbar *(pulpit)*, a Mithrab *(a prayer niche)*, and a minaret *(a tower-like structure)*.

In America the difference between a Masjid and Islamic Center is that a Masjid is usually open for the five daily prayers and an Islamic Center is not usually open for the five daily prayers. They each might provide community programs and activities, run a weekend or daily school, and have a social hall or culture space.

The spelling of the name G-d without the "o" is a tradition of many Jewish people from around the world and a tradition now among many Muslims in America to spell the English translation of the name Allah "G-d" without the "o" because if one spells the name with the "o" it spells the name dog backward and "G-d" the almighty the creator of the heavens and the earth is no dog. Therefore we pick up the rich tradition of not spelling the word "G-d" with the "o" as Imam Warith Deen Mohammed has pointed out and taken the lead in maintaining the best example of our Prophet Muhammad *saw* in respecting and knowing the best of the faith and tradition of the people of the book.

Table of Contents

Masajid (Mosques) and Islamic Centers from Around the Country

Early Mosques in America

One of America's earliest known buildings used for Muslim prayer service was built in 1929, in Ross, North Dakota. In 1902 twenty families moved from Birey, Syria to Ross, North Dakota. By the mid 1970s the community had the building knocked down.

Photo from: A Century of Islam in America: Courtesy of Attiyeh Foundation, WDC

Early Mosques in America

Photo from: 50 Years of Islam in Iowa, Unity Publishing Co. Courtesy of Bill Asi

The Muslim Temple of Cedar Rapids, Iowa was completed in 1934. The Mosque became known as the *"Mother Mosque of America."* Around 1910 a wave of Muslim immigrants from Syria and Lebanon moved to Iowa. By the early 1920s a small group of them started renting a building to serve as a Mosque. They became known as the "The Rose of Fraternity Lodge." Two of the first Imams were Kamil Al-Hind from Damascus and Shaykh Khalil Al-Rawaf from the Najd (in northern Saudi Arabia).

Early Mosques in America

The Minaret of the Islamic Center of Washington, DC

Early Mosques in America

Photo by Amir Muhammad

Islamic Center

The Islamic Center of Washington, DC was built in 1957. The Islamic Center was the first Mosque built in America from the ground up with traditional Islamic architectural structure.

Today there are at least 11 Masajid and Islamic Centers in Washington, DC.

Early Mosques of America

The Mithrab *(prayer niche)* of
Masjid Muhammad, Washington, DC

Early Mosques of America

Masjid Muhammad, of Washington, DC was built in 1960. Masjid Muhammad was the former Muhammad Mosque #4 of the Nation of Islam. Masjid Muhammad was the first Mosque built from the ground up under the leadership of Elijah Muhammad. Today Masjid Muhammad is the Mother Masjid of many of the other Masajid and Islamic Centers in the Washington, DC metropolitan area.

Early Mosques in America

Photo by Amir Muhammad

The Albanian Islamic Center

The Albanian Islamic Center was built in 1962, Harper Wood, Michigan. The Albanian American Muslim Center in Harper Wood was lead by Imam Vehbi Ismail.

Early Mosques in America

Photo by Amir Muhammad

The Albanian Islamic Center

There are at least 76 Masajid and Islamic Centers in the state of Michigan.

Early Mosques in America

Photo by Amir Muhammad

The Albanian American Muslim Community Mosque

The Albanian Mosque and minaret of Waterbury, Connecticut was built in 1965.

Today there are at least 21 Masajid and Islamic Centers in the state of Connecticut.

Chapter 2

Masajid (Mosques) and Islamic Centers of the New England Region

As of 2005 in the New England States, there were at least 68 Masajid (Mosques) and Islamic Centers. There are at least 3 in New Hampshire, 1 in Vermont, 2 in Maine, 9 in Rhode Island, 31 in Massachusetts and 22 in Connecticut.

Resources: Muslim Journal, Connecticut Iqraa Vol. 9-1997, ISNA/FAMTech 1996-97 Islamic Road map, The 1994 Muslim Resource Guide, the Muslim 2002 Yellow Pages, and the 2006 White pages.

Masajid (Mosques) and Islamic Centers of the New England Region

Photo by Amir Muhammad

The Islamic Society of Boston Massachusetts (IBS) was organized in 1982 by Muslim students. In 1993, the society purchased and renovated the current site. They have over 1,000 in attendance at Friday prayers.

The Islamic Society of Boston community is planning to have an open house in 2006 for their new Masjid built from the ground up.

There are at least 31 Masjid and Islamic Centers in Massachusetts.

Masajid (Mosques) and Islamic Centers of the New England Region

The Islamic Center of New England
Quincy, Massachusetts

The Islamic Center in Quincy, Mass is one of the first in New England. Many Muslim immigrants began meeting in the 1930s on South Street in Quincy. By 1962 they started meeting and planning to build an Islamic Center. In 1964 the Center was completed. The membership of the center is approximately 600 people. The center is the oldest Islamic Center in New England.

Masajid (Mosques) and Islamic Centers of the New England Region

Photo by Amir Muhammad

Masjid Al-Quran, Dorchester, Massachusetts

The community of Masjid Al-Quran was founded in the 1940s in Boston's south end as Temple #11 of the Nation of Islam. They moved to this present location in 1958. Both Malcolm X (El-Hajj Malik Shabazz) and Minister Louis Farrakhan ministered and taught at this Masjid.

Masajid (Mosques) and Islamic Centers of the New England Region

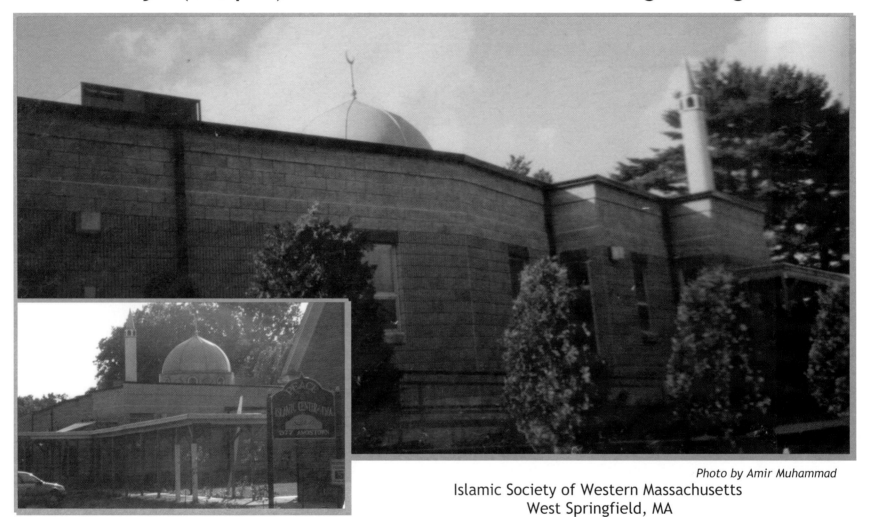

Photo by Amir Muhammad

Islamic Society of Western Massachusetts
West Springfield, MA

The Islamic Society of Western Massachusetts was established in 1982.
The Masjid was completed in 1991.

Masajid (Mosques) and Islamic Centers of the New England Region

Photo Courtesy of Masjid Al-Islam

Masjid Al-Islam, North Smithfield, Rhode Island
Masjid Al-Islam was founded in 1994.

There are at least 9 Masajid and Islamic Centers in Rhode Island.

Masajid (Mosques) and Islamic Centers of the New England Region

Photo by Amir Muhammad

Madina Masjid of the Islamic Center of Connecticut
Windsor, Connecticut was completed in 1993.

There are at least 22 Masajid and Islamic Centers in Connecticut.

Masajid (Mosques) and Islamic Centers of the New England Region

Muhammad Islamic Center of Hartford, Connecticut

US Senator Joseph Liberman visiting Connecticut's Muhammad Islamic Center with the late Imam Qasim.

Photo Courtesy of Muhammad Islamic Center of Hartford

Muhammad Islamic Cultural Center

Photo by Amir Muhammad

Muhammad Islamic Center New Haven, Connecticut.
Muhammad Islamic Center was known formerly as Temple #40 of the Nation of Islam.

Masajid (Mosques) and Islamic Centers of the New England Region

Photo by Amir Muhammad

The Albanian Muslim Community of Waterbury, Connecticut Masjid was built in 1965.

Chapter 3

Masajid and Islamic Centers of the Mid-Atlantic Region

*In the Mid-Atlantic States there are at least 408 Masajid (Mosques) and Islamic Centers.
There are at least 162 in New York, 94 in New Jersey, 57 in Pennsylvania, 4 in Delaware, 37 in Maryland,
11 in Washington, DC, 40 in Virginia, and 3 in West Virginia*

Masajid (Mosques) and Islamic Centers of the Mid Atlantic Region

Masjid Malcolm Shabazz, New York, NY

In the State of New York there are at least 162 Masajid and Islamic Centers. In the Metro area of New York City there are 91 Masajid and Islamic Centers.

References: ISNA / FAMTech 1996 -1997 USA Islamic Roadmap, Masajid & Islamic Centers in Metro NYC, the Philadelphia Masajid As-Shur Masajid list, the Muslim Community Directory of Washington, DC, and the Muslim Yellow pages 2001.

Photos by Amir Muhammad

Masjid Malcolm Shabazz providing Townhouses in the neighborhood

Masjid Malcolm Shabazz Market place

Masajid (Mosques) and Islamic Centers of Mid-Atlantic Region

Photo by Amir Muhammad

Masjid Malcolm Shabazz, New York NY

Masjid Malcolm Shabazz is the former world famous Temple #7 of the Nation of Islam where the late El-Hajj Malik Shabazz (Malcolm X) and Minister Louis Farrakhan use to teach from. The Masjid was renamed by Warith D. Mohammed in 1976 in honor of Malcolm Shabazz. Masjid Malcolm Shabazz in Harlem has grown over the years, including the community around the Masjid. Under the leadership of Imam Izak-el Pasha, the Masjid Malcolm Shabazz community has developed a small business empowerment zone and market place, home ownership with new construction, and rental units to help revitalize the neighborhood.

Masajid (Mosques) and Islamic Centers of Mid-Atlantic Region

Photos by Amir Muhammad

Islamic Center of Manhattan, New York was built in 1993.

Masajid (Mosques) and Islamic Centers of Mid-Atlantic Region

Islamic Mission of America
The "State St. Mosque" Masjid Dawud, Brooklyn New York

Masjid Dawud is better known as the "State Street Mosque," one of the earliest Islamic Centers and Masjid in the New York area. In 1928 Sheikh Al-Hajj Daoud Ahmed Faisal started the Islamic Propagation Center. Sheikh Faisal also started the Islamic Mission Society in 1934.

Photos by Amir Muhammad

Masjid Salaam, New York New York

30

Masajid (Mosques) and Islamic Centers of Mid-Atlantic Region

Photo Courtesy of Riad K. Ali

The Islamic Society of Central New York 'ISCNY'
Syracuse, New York opened July 1981.

Masajid (Mosques) and Islamic Centers of Mid-Atlantic Region

Photo courtesy of Mid-Hudson Islamic Association

Mid-Hudson Islamic Association (MHIA)

The Mid-Hudson Islamic Association organized in the 1960s and their current Masjid was built in 1990. Wappinger, Falls New York.

Masajid (Mosques) and Islamic Centers of Mid-Atlantic Region

Photo Courtesy of the Islamic Center of Rochester

Islamic Center of Rochester New York

The Islamic Center of Rochester was founded in 1975, and current Masjid was built in 1986

Masajid (Mosques) and Islamic Centers of Mid-Atlantic Region

Photo courtesy of Islamic Center of Long Island, N.Y

Islamic Center of Long Island New York

Masajid (Mosques) and Islamic Centers of the Mid-Atlantic Region

Photo by Amir Muhammad

Masjid Muhammad Newark, New Jersey

Newark was also a strong hold for Muslims dating back to the days and followers of Noble Drew Ali in the 1920-30s, and Elijah Muhammad and his followers in the 1950s-1970s. Today Newark, NJ has at least 13 Masajid and Islamic Centers, Jersey City has at least 12 Masajid and Islamic Centers, and Patterson has at least 8 Masajid and Islamic Centers.

In the State of New Jersey there are at least 94 Masjid and Islamic Centers.

Masajid (Mosques) and Islamic Centers of the Mid-Atlantic Region

Masjid Al-Haqq Inc. is dedicated to promoting the lifestyle of Al-Islam, as expressed in the Glorious Quran, and exemplified in the life, actions, and sayings of Prophet Muhammad ibn Abdullah. *(saw)*

Photo by Amir Muhammad

Masjid Al-Haqq, Newark, New Jersey

Masajid (Mosques) and Islamic Centers of the Mid-Atlantic Region

Photo by Amir Muhammad

Al-Tawheed Islamic Center
Jersey City, New Jersey

Masajid (Mosques) and Islamic Centers of the Mid-Atlantic Region

Photo by Amir Muhammad

Masjid Dar Ul-Islam in
Teaneck, New Jersey was completed in 1986.

Masajid (Mosques) and Islamic Centers of the Mid-Atlantic Region

Islamic Society of Central Jersey

In 1975 the ISC was incorporated as a non-profit organization. In 1977 a merger between two area Islamic communities from the greater New Brunswick, Princeton, and Trenton areas came together to form the Islamic Society of Central Jersey ISCJ. In 1979 they purchased 6.4 acres in South Brunswick. By 1982 the community began their first phase of the Center which was the school and multipurpose hall. This phase was completed by 1983. The second phase was started in 1988 and completed by 1990. At present there are more than 2,000 families on the Masjid mailing list.

Masajid (Mosques) and Islamic Centers of Mid-Atlantic Region

Photo by Amir Muhammad

Masjid Ibraheem

The Islamic Society of Delaware was established in 1975. In 1991 the community bought a Masjid, and since then the community has outgrown their current space and are preparing to add a new addition.

Masjid Ibraheem

Today there are at least 4 Islamic Centers and Masajid in the state of Delaware.

Masajid (Mosques) and Islamic Centers of Mid-Atlantic Region

Photos by Amir Muhammad

Masjidullah
Philadelphia, Pennsylvania

*Today there are at least 57 Islamic Centers and Masajid in the state of Pennsylvania.
In the city of Philadelphia there are at least 23 Masajid and Centers and the city of Pittsburgh is home to
at least 7 Masajid and Islamic Centers.*

41

Masajid (Mosques) and Islamic Centers of Mid-Atlantic Region

Photo by Amir Muhammad

Masjid Bawa Muhaiyuddeed, Philadelphia, Pennsylvania

Masjid Bawa Muhaiyuddeed was open in May 1984.

Masajid (Mosques) and Islamic Centers of Mid-Atlantic Region

Photo by Amir Muhammad

The Islamic Center of Pittsburgh, Pennsylvania

The Islamic Center of Pittsburgh is the area's largest Mosque, providing services to both Muslims and non Muslims.

Masajid (Mosques) and Islamic Centers of Mid-Atlantic Region

Photo by Amir Muhammad

Masjid Al-Awwal, Pittsburgh, PA

The First Muslim Mosque of Pennsylvania was established in 1932 in Pittsburgh.

Masajid (Mosques) and Islamic Centers of Mid-Atlantic Region

Photo by Amir Muhammad

Muslim Community Center of Greater Pittsburgh
Monroeville, Pennsylvania

45

Masajid (Mosques) and Islamic Centers of Mid-Atlantic Region

Photo by Amir Muhammad

Masjid Al-Haqq, Baltimore, MD

Masjid Al-Haqq was one of the earliest Masajid in the state of Maryland. Masjid Al-Haqq's early followers were members of the Nation of Islam in the 1940-1970s.

Today there are at least 37 Islamic Centers and Masajid in the State of Maryland.

Masajid (Mosques) and Islamic Centers of Mid-Atlantic Region

Photo by Amir Muhammad

The Islamic Center of Southern Maryland of
Prince Fredrick, Maryland was completed in 1986.

Masajid (Mosques) and Islamic Centers of Mid-Atlantic Region

Photos by Amir Muhammad

Masjid Bait Ur Rehman, Silver Spring, Maryland

Masajid (Mosques) and Islamic Centers of Mid-Atlantic Region

Masjid Bait Ur Rahman, Silver Spring, Maryland

The Masjid sits on 10 acres outside of Washington, DC and functions as a Mosque, administrate offices, and social complex.

Masajid (Mosques) and Islamic Centers of Mid-Atlantic Region

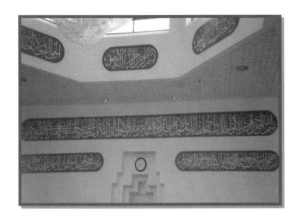

Photos by Amir Muhammad

Muslim Community Center (MCC)
Silver Spring, Maryland

Masajid (Mosques) and Islamic Centers of Mid-Atlantic Region

Dar Al Hijrah Islamic Center

Photos by Amir Muhammad

Dar Al Hijrah Islamic Center of Falls Church, Virginia beginnings date back to 1983 when they first came together. The Masjid construction began in 1986 and was completed March 1991. Today the Masjid serves more than 5,000 Muslims in the area.

Today there are at least 51 Islamic Centers and Masajid in the State of Virginia.

All Dulles Area Muslim Society (ADAMS)
Sterling, Virginia

ADAMS was established in 1983 by a small, group of Muslim families from the Herndon/ Reston area of Northern Virginia. Today ADAMS Center serves 5,000 families in the area. The Center has a Masjid, Weekend School for 500 children, a community multi-purpose hall, library, and a gym.

Photo by Amir Muhammad

Masajid (Mosques) and Islamic Centers of Mid-Atlantic Region

Photo by Amir Muhammad

The Mustafa Center
In Annandale, Virginia

The Mustafa Center was completed in 1999.

Masajid (Mosques) and Islamic Centers of Mid-Atlantic Region

Photo by Amir Muhammad

The Islamic Center of Virginia
Richmond Virginia

The Islamic Center of Virginia was completed in 1990.
The Islamic Center is a non-profit organization serving the needs of Muslims in Central Virginia.

Masajid (Mosques) and Islamic Centers of Mid-Atlantic Region

Photo by Amir Muhammad

Al-Quba Islamic Center, Newport News, Virginia

Al-Quba was one of the first Masajid in the Newport News area dating back to the early days of the former Nation of Islam.

Masajid (Mosques) and Islamic Centers of Mid-Atlantic Region

Photos by Amir Muhammad

The Mosque and Islamic Center of Hampton Roads
Hampton, Virginia

Masajid (Mosques) and Islamic Centers of Mid-Atlantic Region

The Islamic Center of Charleston West Virginia
The West Virginia Islamic Center was constructed in 1987.

Photos from the Collections of CSAM

Today there are at least 3 Masajid and Islamic Centers in the state of West Virginia.

Chapter 4

Masajid and Islamic Centers of the Southeastern and South Central Region

In the Southeastern and South Central Region there are at least 374 Masajid (Mosques) and Islamic Centers. There are at least 50 in North Carolina, 14 in South Carolina, 52 in Georgia, 47 in Florida, 23 in Alabama, 21 in Tennessee, 9 in Arkansas, 10 in Mississippi, 31 in Louisiana, 16 in Oklahoma, and at least 101 in Texas.

References: Muslim Journal, Masjid As-Shur of North Carolina, Muslim Resource Guide 1994, ISNA 1996 Road Map of Islamic Centers, Islamicity.com, Salatomatic, and the Pluralism Project

Masajid (Mosques) and Islamic Centers of the Southeastern Region

Masjid Omar ibn Sayyid, Fayetteville, North Carolina

The first Masjid Omar Ibn Sayyid was built in 1986, in Fayetteville, NC. The Masjid is named after Omar ibn Sayyid who was one of the better known and scholarly enslaved Muslims of the American slavery period. Members of this Masjid are among the few communities in America who have built two Masajid from the ground up. The second Masjid was completed in 2000.

The first Masjid Omar

Today there are at least 50 Masajid and Islamic Centers in the State of North Carolina.

Photo by Amir Muhammad

Ar-Razzaq Islamic Center, Durham, North Carolina

The Ar-Razzaq Islamic Center was established in the early 1970s. In the early days of the community they were with the Nation of Islam and were known as Temple #34. Today in the city of Durham there are five Masajid and Islamic Centers.

Masajid (Mosques) and Islamic Centers of the Southeastern Region

Masjid Al-Muminun, Winston Salem

Masjid Al-Muminun is one of the earliest Masajid in the city of Winston-Salem and today there are a total of four Masajid and Islamic Centers in the city.

Masajid (Mosques) and Islamic Centers of the Southeastern Region

Photo by Amir Muhammad

The Islamic Center of Charlotte, North Carolina

Both the cities of Charlotte and Greensboro are home to the largest number of Masajid and Islamic Centers in the state of North Carolina with six each.

Masajid (Mosques) and Islamic Centers of the Southeastern Region

Photo by Amir Muhammad

Masjid Al-Jami Ar-Rasheed
Charleston, South Carolina

Today there are at least 14 Masajid and Islamic Centers in the State of South Carolina.

Masajid (Mosques) and Islamic Centers of the Southeastern Region

Photo courtesy of the Pluralism Project Archives

Masjid Al-Muslimin/ the Islamic Center of Columbia

The Islamic Center of Columbia was formed in 1982 and in 1993 they built their current Masjid.

Masajid (Mosques) and Islamic Centers of the Southeastern Region

Photo by Amir Muhammad

Al-Huda Islamic Center Athens, Georgia

Al-Huda Islamic Center of Athens in Georgia was started in 1981 among a group of foreign Muslim students. In 1987 they completed the new building they are currently in.

Today there are at least 53 Masajid and Islamic Centers in the State of Georgia.

Masajid (Mosques) and Islamic Centers of the Southeastern Region

Photo by Amir Muhammad

Atlanta Masjid of Al-Islam,
Atlanta, Georgia

The Atlanta Masjid is one of the oldest Masjid in Georgia. The community was founded by the late Honorable Elijah Muhammad in 1958. In 1989-90 the community purchased and renovated the current Masjid and the strip mall business complex.

Today in the Atlanta metropolitan area there are at least 28 Islamic Centers and Masajid.

Masajid (Mosques) and Islamic Centers of the Southeastern Region

Photo by Amir Muhammad

Masjid Jihad, Savannah, Georgia

Masajid (Mosques) and Islamic Centers of the Southeastern Region

The Islamic Center of Northeast Florida
Jacksonville, Florida

The Islamic Center of Northeast Florida
was incorporated as a non-profit
organization in 1978.

Photo by Amir Muhammad

Today there are at least 47 Masajid and Islamic Centers in the State of Florida.

Masajid (Mosques) and Islamic Centers of the Southeastern Region

Photo by Amir Muhammad

Masjid Al-Ansar
Miami, Florida

Masjid Al-Ansar is one of the oldest Masjid in South Florida, together with Masjid Ibrahim. Masjid Al-Ansar was purchased in 1968. The early members of the community were members of the old Nation of Islam.

Masajid (Mosques) and Islamic Centers of the Southeastern Region

Masjid Miami Garden, Miami Florida   *Photo by Amir Muhammad*

Masjid Miami Gardens' community came together in 1973 and two years later they purchased a house and turned it into a Masjid. By 1991 they started building their current site which was completed in 1997. In both the cities of Miami and Tampa there are six Masajid and Islamic Centers, followed by the cities of Jacksonville and Gainesville, which both have three Masajid and Islamic Centers.

Masajid (Mosques) and Islamic Centers of the Southeastern Region

Photo by Amir Muhammad

Masjid Omar ibn ul Kattab, Tuscaloosa Islamic Center
Tuscaloosa, Alabama

Today there are at least 22 Masajid and Islamic Centers in the State of Alabama.

Masajid (Mosques) and Islamic Centers of the Southeastern Region

Photo Courtesy of Huntsville Islamic Center

Huntsville Islamic Center, Huntsville, Alabama

In both the cities of Huntsville and Mobile there are three Masajid and Islamic Centers, and in the cities of Birmingham and Tuscaloosa there are two Masajid and Islamic Centers.

Masajid (Mosques) and Islamic Centers of the Southeastern Region

Islamic Center of Nashville

Photo by Amir Muhammad

The Islamic Center of Nashville, Tennessee was founded in 1978 and in March 1989 they completed their new Masjid.

Today there are at least 21 Masajid and Islamic Centers in the State of Tennessee.

Masajid (Mosques) and Islamic Centers of the Southeastern Region

Masjid As-Salaam / the Muslim Society of Memphis   *Photo by Amir Muhammad*

The Muslim Society of Memphis was founded in 1978. In 1980 the society purchased a small house for the Masjid.
By 1984 the society outgrew the house and built their current Masjid.

Masajid (Mosques) and Islamic Centers of the Southeastern Region

Masjid An-Nur, Memphis, Tennessee

Photos by Amir Muhammad

In the cities of Memphis and Knoxville there are five Masajid and Islamic Centers.
The city of Nashville has six Masajid and Islamic Centers.

Masajid (Mosques) and Islamic Centers of the South Central Region

Photo courtesy of the Pluralism Project Archives

The Masjid of Oxford Muslim Society

The Masjid of the Oxford Muslim Society was built in Oxford, Mississippi in 1999 near
the campus of the University of Mississippi.

Today there are at least 21 Masajid and Islamic Centers in the State of Mississippi.

Masajid (Mosques) and Islamic Centers of the South Central Region

Masjid Muhammad, Jacksonville, Mississippi   *Photo by Amir Muhammad*

Masjid Muhammad is one of the oldest Masjid in the state of Mississippi
which dates back to the old Nation of Islam of the 70s.

Masajid (Mosques) and Islamic Centers of the South Central Region

Photo courtesy of the Islamic Center of Mississippi

The Islamic Center of Mississippi

The Islamic Center of Mississippi in Starkville, MS was built in 1992 near the campus of Mississippi State.

Masajid (Mosques) and Islamic Centers of the South Central Region

Photo Courtesy of Habeebah Muhammad

Masjidur Raheem,
New Orleans, Louisiana

Today there are at least 23 Masajid and Islamic Centers in the State of Louisiana.

Masajid (Mosques) and Islamic Centers of the South Central Region

Photo Courtesy of the Islamic Society of Greater Houston

Masjid Bilal, Islamic Society of Greater Houston North Zone Mosque
Houston, Texas

The Islamic Society of Greater of Houston was incorporated in 1969. The ISGH provides educational, religious, social, and cultural services for the community. Today the community serves more than 50,000 people a year. There are sixteen Masajid and Islamic Centers in the Greater Houston area.

Today there are at least 101 Masajid and Islamic Centers in the State of Texas

Masajid (Mosques) and Islamic Centers of the South Central Region

Photo Courtesy of Habeebah Muhammad

Masjid Al-Islam, Dallas, Texas

The Dallas Masjid of Al-Islam started out as Mosque #48 in the former Nation of Islam around 1968. In 1980 the community purchased their current Masjid.

Masajid (Mosques) and Islamic Centers of the South Central Region

Photo Courtesy of the Islamic Society of Greater Houston

Masjid Attaqwa, Islamic Society of Greater Houston Southwest Zone Mosque
Sugarland, Texas

In the greater metropolitan area of the city of Dallas there are at least thirteen Masajid and Islamic Centers and in the greater Houston metro area there are at least fourteen Masajid and Islamic Centers.

Masajid (Mosques) and Islamic Centers of the South Central Region

Photo Courtesy of the Islamic Society of Greater Houston

Masjid Ar-Rahman, Baytown Mosque
Islamic Society of Greater Houston Southeast Zone (ISGH)
Baytown, Texas

Masajid (Mosques) and Islamic Centers of the South Central Region

Photo Courtesy of the Islamic Center of Irving Texas

Islamic Center of Irving, Texas

The Islamic Center of Irving was established in 1991. In 1998 they purchased 11 acres of land and by 1999 they started building the new Masjid. In 2004 the Masjid held its grand opening.

Masajid (Mosques) and Islamic Centers of the South Central Region

Photo by Riad k. Ali courtesy of Al-Anwar

Islamic Association of Mid Cities, Colleyville, Texas

Masajid (Mosques) and Islamic Centers of the South Central Region

Photo by Riad k. Ali courtesy of Al-Anwar

Masjid An-Nasr, Islamic Association of Greater Oklahoma City,
Oklahoma City, Oklahoma

Today there are at least 16 Masajid and Islamic Centers in the State of Oklahoma.

Chapter 5

Masajid and Islamic Centers of the Great Lakes and North Central Region

In the Great Lakes and North Central Region there are at least 330 Masajid (Mosques) and Islamic Centers, at least 50 in Ohio, 76 in Michigan, 22 in Indiana, 81 in Illinois, 19 in Wisconsin, 14 in Minnesota, 14 in Iowa, 13 in Missouri, 19 in Kentucky, 12 in Kansas, 4 in Nebraska, 3 in South Dakota, and at least 3 in North Dakota.

References: Muslim Journal, Muslim 1994 Resource Directory, Muslim Yellow Pages 2001, ISNA 1996 Road Map of Islamic Centers, Islamicity.com, Salatomatic, and the Pluralism Project

Masajid and Islamic Centers of the Great Lakes and North Central Region

Photo by Amir Muhammad

The Islamic Center of Greater Toledo, Perrysburg, Ohio

In 1954 the community built Toledo's first Islamic Center, near downtown Toledo on East Bancroft. In 1978 they purchased forty-eight acres in Perrysburg. The Masjid was built in 1983 with two new wings added on in 1991.

Today there are at least 50 Masajid and Islamic Centers in the state of Ohio.

Masajid and Islamic Centers of the Great Lakes and North Central Region

Photos by Amir Muhammad

The Islamic Center of Greater Toledo, Perrysburg, Ohio.

Photo by Amir Muhammad

Masjid Bilal, Cleveland, Ohio

Masjid Bilal community dates back to the early days of 1950s in the Nation of Islam in the Cleveland area. Masjid Bilal was built in 1983. It was the first Masjid built under the new leadership of Imam W. Deen Mohammed.

Cleveland leads the state with twelve Masajid and Islamic Centers, followed by the cities of Cincinnati and Columbus who each have six Masajid and Islamic Centers.

Photo by Amir Muhammad

Islamic Center of Central Ohio
Columbus, Ohio

Masajid and Islamic Centers of the Great Lakes and North Central Region

Photo courtesy of the Grand Mosque

The Grand Mosque, Islamic Center of Cleveland

The Islamic Center of Cleveland was founded in 1967. The community built and completed the current Masjid in 1995.

Masajid and Islamic Centers of the Great Lakes and North Central Region

American Muslim Society's first building

American Muslim Society   *Photo by Amir Muhammad*

The American Muslim Society Mosque was established in 1937. It is the oldest Masjid in the state of Michigan. In 1952 the Mosque was expanded and in 2000 the Masjid was expanded to double in size.

Today there are at least 76 Masajid and Islamic Centers in the state of Michigan.

Photo by Amir Muhammad

Detroit Masjid, Detroit, Michigan

Today in the city of Detroit there at least 21 Masajid and Islamic Centers, followed next by Dearborn which has 11 Masajid and Islamic Centers. The next city with a large amount of Masajid and Islamic Centers is Hamtramck, Michigan with 6, followed by Flint and Grand Rapids with 3 each.

Photo by Amir Muhammad

Masjid Wali Muhammad, Detroit, Michigan

Masjid Wali Muhammad was formerly known as Temple #1 in the early days of the Nation of Islam until the mid 70's when the community changed and began following the Sunnah under the leadership of the son of Elijah Muhammad, Imam Warith Deen Mohammed.

Islamic Center of America, Detroit, Michigan

The Islamic Center of America is one of the oldest Islamic institutions in America which begun to form in the 1940s. On September 20, 1963 the center opened its doors and by 1967 the Center was enlarged. The community today is currently planning to build a new larger Masjid.

Masajid and Islamic Centers of the Great Lakes and North Central Region

Photo by Amir Muhammad

The Islamic Center of America
Detroit, Michigan

Masajid and Islamic Centers of the Great Lakes and North Central Region

Photo by Amir Muhammad

The Albanian Islamic Center
Harper Woods, Michigan

The Albanian Islamic Center was founded in 1962.

Masajid and Islamic Centers of the Great Lakes and North Central Region

The Muslim Community Association of Ann Arbor.
Ann Arbor, Michigan

Photos by Amir Muhammad

Masjid Al-Fajr, Indianapolis, Indiana

In the state of Indiana five of its cities have 3 Masajid and Islamic Centers which are Fort Wayne, South Bend, Gary, Michigan City, and Indianapolis.

Photos by Amir Muhammad

Today there are at least 22 Masajid and Islamic Centers in the state of Indiana.

Masajid and Islamic Centers of the Great Lakes and North Central Region

Photo by Amir Muhammad

Masjid Al-Amin
Gary, Indiana

Photo by Amir Muhammad

Islamic Dawah Center
South Bend, Indiana

Masajid and Islamic Centers of the Great Lakes and North Central Region

The Islamic Society of North America (ISNA) / Masjid

The Islamic Society of North America's (ISNA)
current building was completed in 1979.

Photo by Amir Muhammad

Photo by Amir Muhammad

The Islamic Center of Bloomington
Bloomington, Indiana

The Islamic Center of Bloomington was established in the mid 1970s. In 1983 the community purchased some land and in 1993 the community built their current Masjid from the ground up.

Masajid and Islamic Centers of the Great Lakes and North Central Region

Photo courtesy of and by Riad K. Ali

The Islamic Community Center of Des Plaines
Des Plaines, Illinois

Today there are at least 81 Masajid and Islamic Centers in the state of Illinois.

Masajid and Islamic Centers of the Great Lakes and North Central Region

Photos by Amir Muhammad

The Mosque Foundation
Bridgeview, Illinois

The Mosque Foundation was established in 1967 and opened its doors in 1981. Today the Masjid is one of the largest Masjid in the Mid-west.

Masajid and Islamic Centers of the Great Lakes and North Central Region

Photo by Amir Muhammad

Masjid Al-Faatir, Chicago, Illinois

Masjid Al-Faatir was opened in 1987 as the first Masjid in the city of Chicago built from the ground up. The world famous Heavyweight Champion Muhammad Ali and Herbert Muhammad, the son of the Honorable Elijah Muhammad helped finance the building of the Masjid.

Masajid and Islamic Centers of the Great Lakes and North Central Region

Masjid Al-Faatir, Chicago, Illinois

Photos by Amir Muhammad

Within the city limits of Chicago there are at least 34 Masajid and Islamic Centers.

Masajid and Islamic Centers of the Great Lakes and North Central Region

Photo by Amir Muhammad

The Islamic Foundation was established in 1974 in the suburbs of Chicago to fulfill the Muslim Community's religious, educational, and cultural needs. The current Masjid and School was completed in 1998.

The Islamic Foundation
Villa Park, Illinois

Masajid and Islamic Centers of the Great Lakes and North Central Region

Photo Courtesy of Masjid-e-Ihsan

Masjid e-Ihsan Islamic Center of the Quad Cities
Moline, Illinois

The Islamic Center of the Quad Cities was founded in the 1980s and the new Masjid was completed in 2005.

Masajid and Islamic Centers of the Great Lakes and North Central Region

Photo courtesy of Masjid Tawheed of the Albanian American Islamic Society

Masjid Tawheed, Albanian American Islamic Society
Kenosha, Wisconsin

The city of Milwaukee has at least six Masajid and Islamic Centers followed by the cities of Appleton, Racine, Madison, and Kenosha with two each.

Today there are at least 19 Masajid and Islamic Centers in the state of Wisconsin.

Masajid and Islamic Centers of the Great Lakes and North Central Region

Photos courtesy of Islamic Cultural Heritage Center

Islamic Cultural Heritage Center of America "The Mother Mosque," Cedar Rapid's, Iowa.
On June 16, 1934 the "Mother Mosque" the first Islamic house of prayer was open in Cedar Rapids.

Today there are at least 14 Masajid and Islamic Centers in the state of Iowa.

Masajid and Islamic Centers of the Great Lakes and North Central Region

Islamic Center of Cedar Rapids, Iowa

Photo Courtesy of Bill Asi from: 50 Years of Islam in Iowa

The current Masjid was built and opened in 1972.

Masajid and Islamic Centers of the Great Lakes and North Central Region

Photo by Habeebah Muhammad

The Islamic Center of Greater St. Louis
St. Louis, Missouri

Today in the City of St. Louis there are at least eight Masajid and Islamic Centers
followed by Kansas City with three Masajid and Islamic Center each.

Today there are at least 18 Masajid and Islamic Centers in the state of Missouri.

Masajid and Islamic Centers of the Great Lakes and North Central Region

Photo by Habeebah Muhammad

Masjid An-Noor of the Islamic Society of Wichita.
Wichita, Kansas

Today there are at least 12 Masajid and Islamic Centers in the state of Kansas.

Masajid and Islamic Centers of the Great Lakes and North Central Region

One of America's first Muslim House of Prayer, Ross, North Dakota

This building was built and used as a Masjid in the mid 1930s-1960s.

The new Masjid in Ross, North Dakota was completed in 2005 on the same grounds where the old Masjid was built in the 1930s.

The New Masjid in Ross, North Dakota

Today there are at least 4 Masajid and Islamic Centers in the state of North Dakota.

Chapter 6

Masajid and Islamic Centers of the Western Region
Fours Corners, and the Northwestern, and Southwestern

In the Western region Fours Corners, Northwestern, and Southwestern there are at least 307 Masajid (Mosques) and Islamic Centers. At least 16 in Arizona, 7 in New Mexico, 17 in Colorado, 6 in Utah, 34 in Washington, 5 in Idaho, 2 in Montana, 2 in Wyoming, 14 in Oregon, 4 in Nevada, and 200 in California.

Resources: Muslim Journal, Muslim 1994 Resource Directory, Muslim Yellow Pages 2001, ISNA 1996 Road Map of Islamic Centers, IslamicValley, Salatomatic, Islamicity.com, and the Pluralism Project

Masajid and Islamic Centers of Four Corners, and the North and South Western Region

Photo Courtesy of Tucson Islamic Center

Islamic Center of Tucson
Tucson, Arizona

The Islamic Center of Tucson was established in 1966, and the current Masjid was completed in 1990.

Today there are at least 16 Masajid and Islamic Centers in the state of Arizona.

Photo Courtesy of Tucson Islamic Center

Islamic Community Center
Tempe, Arizona

The student dominated Masjid was established in 1984 just north of the campus of Arizona State University.

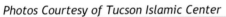

Photos Courtesy of Tucson Islamic Center

Islamic Community Center of Tempe, Arizona.

Masajid and Islamic Centers of Four Corners, and the North and South Western Region

Photo courtesy of the Islamic Association of Carrollton

Islamic Association of Carrollton
Carrollton, Arizona

The Islamic Association of Carrollton Masjid was opened September 2005.

In the city of Phoenix there are at least eight Masajid and Islamic Centers, followed by the cities of Tempe and Tucson with two Masajid and Islamic Centers each.

Masajid and Islamic Centers of Four Corners, and the North and South Western Region

Masjid Dar- Al-Islam
Abiquiu, New Mexico

Photo courtesy of Masjid Dar-Islam

Dar-al-Islam was incorporated in the 1970s, and the Masjid was completed in 1989.

Today there are at least 7 Masajid and Islamic Centers in the State of New Mexico.

Photo Courtesy of Masjid Khadijah

Masjid Khadijah
Taos, New Mexico

Photo Courtesy of Colorado Muslim Society

Masjid Abu-Baker, Colorado Muslim Society
Denver, Colorado

Today there are at least 17 Masajid and Islamic Centers in the State of Colorado.

Masajid and Islamic Centers of Four Corners, and the North and South Western Region

Photo Courtesy of Islamic Center of Boulder

Islamic Center of Boulder, Colorado

The Islamic Center of Boulder was founded in the 1970s by a group of college students.

Masajid and Islamic Centers of Four Corners, and the North and South Western Region

Photo Courtesy of Masjid Noor Islamic Center

Masjid Noor Islamic Center,
Salt Lake City, Utah

Today there are at least 6 Masajid and Islamic Centers in the State of Utah.

Masajid and Islamic Centers of Four Corners, and the North and South Western Region

Photo Courtesy of Khadeeja Islamic Center

Khadeeja Islamic Center, Salt Lake City, Utah

There are at least three Masajid and Islamic Centers in the city of Salt Lake.

Photo Courtesy of Boise Islamic Center

Islamic Center of Boise, Idaho

In 1982 the first community of Muslims in Boise was formed. In 2002 they purchased their existing Masjid.

Today there are at least 5 Masajid and Islamic Centers in the State of Idaho.

Masajid and Islamic Centers of Four Corners, and the North and South Western Region

Photo courtesy of Masjid As-Sabr, Islamic Center of Portland

Masjid As-Sabr, Islamic Center of Portland

The Masjid As-Sabr community dates back to the early 1970s with students
from the local university. The current Masjid site was completed in 1998.

Today there are at least 14 Masajid and Islamic Centers in the State of Oregon.

Photo by Amir Muhammad

Idris Mosque of the Islamic Center of Seattle
Seattle, Washington

Today there are at least 34 Masajid and Islamic Centers in the State of Washington.

Masajid and Islamic Centers of Four Corners, and the North and South Western Region

Photos by Amir Muhammad

In the greater Settle area there are at least thirteen Masajid and Islamic Centers.

Idris Mosque of the Islamic Center of Seattle, Washington

Masajid and Islamic Centers of Four Corners, and the North and South Western Region

Photo courtesy of the Masjid Omar ibn Al-Khattab

Masjid Omar ibn Al-Khattab, Los Angeles, California

Masjid Omar was opened in Los Angeles January 1994. In the city of Los Angeles there are at least 19 Masajid and Islamic Centers. In the city of San Diego there are 13 Masajid and Islamic Centers, and in the cities of San Francisco and Oakland they each have 9 Masajid and Islamic Centers. The cities of San Jose and Sacramento have 6 each, followed by Pomona with 5 and the cities of Concord, Fremont, and Stockton with 4 each.

Masajid and Islamic Centers of the Four Corners, North and South Western Region

Photo courtesy of the Mosque of Riverside

Mosque of Riverside
Riverside, California

Today there are at least 200 Masajid and Islamic Centers in the State of California.

Masajid and Islamic Centers of Four Corners, and the North and South Western Region

Photo courtesy of Islamic Society of East Bay

Islamic Society of the East Bay
Fremont, California

The community in Fremont is currently building a new Masjid from the ground up.

Masajid and Islamic Centers of Four Corners, and the North and South Western Region

Photo courtesy of Al-Anwar Designs, Riad K. Ali

Islamic Center of San Diego,
San Diego, California

The Islamic Center of San Diego (ICSD) was completed in 1989.

Photo by Habeebah Muhammad

Islamic Foundation, King Fahad Mosque
Culver City, California

Masajid and Islamic Centers of Four Corners, and the North and South Western Region

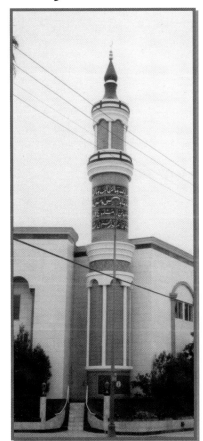

Photos by Habeebah Muhammad

The King Fahd Mosque was opened July 1998.

The Islamic Foundation and King Fahd Mosque

Masajid and Islamic Centers of Four Corners, and the North and South Western Region

Photo courtesy of Islamic Center of Yuba City

Islamic Center of Yuba City, California

In 1994 the building was set on fire and reduced to ruins, but by 2001 the new Masjid was completed.

Chapter 7

Masajid and Islamic Centers off the Main Land of America And within the Muslim American Association

There are at least 10 Masajid and Islamic Centers,
1 in Hawaii, 3 in Alaska, 1 in St. Thomas, 1 in St. Croix, and 4 in Bermuda.

Resources: IslamicValley, Islamicity.com, Pluralism Project, and Salatomatic

Masajid and Islamic Centers within Muslim American Association

Photo by Amir Muhammad

Masjid Nur, Islamic Center of St. Thomas
St. Thomas US Virgin Island

Masajid and Islamic Centers within Muslim American Association

Photo by Amir Muhammad

Masjid Muhammad, Bermuda

This Masjid had its early beginning with the Nation of Islam in the States and made the change with the community in the mid 1970s to follow the Sunnah of Al-Islam. Imam Warith Deen Mohammed, the son of Elijah Muhammad gave the community a large contribution to help purchase this current Masjid.

Today there are at least 4 Islamic Centers or Masajid in Bermuda.